Creating Family Traditions

Making Memories in Festive Seasons

GLORIA GAITHER & SHIRLEY DOBSON

Artwork by Carrie Hartman

Multnomah Gifts®
Multnomah® Publishers *Sisters, Oregon*

CREATING FAMILY TRADITIONS

© 2004 by Gloria Gaither and James Dobson, Inc.
published by Multnomah Gifts®,
a division of Multnomah® Publishers, Inc.
P.O. Box 1720, Sisters, Oregon 97759

International Standard Book Number: 1-59052-341-5

Design by Koechel Peterson, & Assoc., Inc., Minneapolis, Minnesota

Artwork © 2004 by Carrie Hartman
www.carriehartman.com

Unless otherwise indicated, Scripture quotations are taken from:

The Holy Bible, New International Version
©1973, 1984 by International Bible Society,
used by permission of Zondervan Publishing House

Multnomah Publishers, Inc., has made every effort to provide proper and accurate source attribution for all selections used in this book. Should any attribution be found to be incorrect, the publisher welcomes written documentation supporting correction for subsequent printings. We gratefully acknowledge the cooperation of other publishers and individuals who have granted permission for use of their material.

Multnomah is a trademark of Multnomah Publishers, Inc., and is registered in the U.S. Patent and Trademark Office. The colophon is a trademark of Multnomah Publishers, Inc.

Printed in Belgium

For Information:
MULTNOMAH PUBLISHERS, INC. • P.O. BOX 1720 • SISTERS, OR 97759

04 05 06 07 08 09 10 11—10 9 8 7 6 5 4 3 2 1 0

To Madeleine
who is a party all by herself,
but is always happy to have someone
(like her mamaw) join her.

GLORIA GAITHER

This book is
affectionately dedicated to
my husband, Jim Dobson, and to our children,
Danae and Ryan,
with whom we are sharing a lifetime
of priceless memories.

SHIRLEY DOBSON

Table of Contents

Was it the farmhouse smelling of wood smoke and pumpkin pies? Was it the sound of the pump organ or guitar, piano or harmonica? Was it the crunch of snow underfoot or the corn shucks leaning into each other in the fields? Was it the candles in the windows or the happy voices of the whole clan playing dominos, Rook, or Pit around the kitchen table after supper?

Was it using mother's best sewing scissors to cut pink, red, and white hearts out of construction paper or snowflakes out of tissue; was it carving jack-o-lanterns, stringing cranberries and popcorn, cutting bunny-shaped cookies out of fresh sugar dough, or sitting around a bonfire, giggling at wisecracks and singing songs, silly and serious, to the strum of a guitar?

What made home the place to which your heart needed to return? What made Christmas or Easter or Thanksgiving? Or maybe, for you, all the seasons and holidays are just a hungry longing for something you had only heard about in other people's songs and other children's stories.

This book is for you. It's for you because memories have to be made good and precious *on purpose*. It's for you because the holidays may be printed on the calendar but you have to make them meaningful and sacred by being truly *reverent* and actually *present* and intentionally *joyful.* "Meaningful" can't be printed in calendar ink. Treasured memories don't necessarily result from declaring a national holiday and they can't be abolished by eradicating them, either.

"Going on holiday" isn't the same thing as celebrating Christmas. Having "turkey day" is not the same as truly celebrating our national heritage and giving thanks. *Easter* is not the same as spring break. Symbols are symbolic of *something.* Easter eggs, Christmas trees, Seder candles, the American "stars and stripes," the Thanksgiving pilgrims and turkey are only meaningful if we parents and grand-parents, aunts and uncles make them so and keep them so by never tiring of "telling the story." It's all about the story and your special *telling of it* and *living of it.* Without that, sacred moments will crumble into, well, merely trinkets and a day off.

A Word from
Shirley Dobson

When Gloria and I sat down many years ago to write the original manuscript for *Let's Make a Memory*, it was our desire to share some ideas and offer encouragement to families about the importance of making memories together. It was a labor of love, and one that came from deep within our hearts. At that time we still had children at home and were enjoying the hubbub of family life to the full. Many of the suggestions we put forward in that first book were a reflection of our experiences as moms who were engaged in the prime-time responsibilities of parenting. What a wonderful era that was, full of laughter and excitement and the youthful exuberance of childhood.

Though we knew it was designed by God to be a very brief season, we were shocked by how quickly it ended. Those years passed through our hands like a well-greased string, which seemed to move even more rapidly as we tried to hold on. Before we knew it, we were sending our kids off to college, and then learning to adjust to the silence of the empty nest. Now our parenting responsibilities are over, and what remains are the cherished memories that were carefully constructed during those precious years. We have no regrets, because we succeeded in capturing something eternal in the midst of that which was all too temporary.

Today, when Jim and I visit with our grown children, Danae and Ryan, we often reminisce warmly about the fun things we did as a family and the activities that brought us together. The skiing trips, bike rides, Sunday dinners, Christmas mornings, picnic outings, table games, and church experiences remain unchanged and vibrant somewhere within. They reside, as the lyrics of an old Glen Campbell song puts it, "on the back roads, by the river of my memory… And for hours, [they're] just gentle on my mind." What a marvelous place that is.

I agree emphatically with Gloria that the highlights of a lifetime, including the few honors and achievements that have come our way, pale in comparison to the shared experiences that cemented us together during those younger days. The love that grew from them still burns brightly in our hearts today. In fact, our daughter, Danae, has such warm memories of those early days in our family that she speaks regularly at mother-daughter banquets and gatherings on the importance of capturing the moments that matter most.

As we prepare this newest book about memories, we are driven by a passion to urge young families, and grandparents as well, to make time for the traditions and activities that will shine like gold in the days to come. I know it is difficult to give priority to such things. The pace of living is even more frantic now than it was twenty years ago, and many families feel strangled by unrelenting pressures, obligations, and responsibilities. You are probably suffering from the same dilemma. And those of you who are single parents are likely to be even more stressed.

Given those pressures, how can you get away for a Little League game, a pumpkin carving, or a piano recital when a never ending to-do list looms above? How can Dad sit down and work a jigsaw puzzle or build a go-cart or take a fishing trip when the boss expects to get every ounce of his time and energy? How can parents plan and participate in fun things with kids when the roof needs fixing and the monthly checks have to be written and the tires on the car need replacing? The answer is, I don't know. It is never easy to control the demands of living. I am convinced, however, that those who let these and other temporal cares squeeze out memorable family activities will regret it in the days to come.

Traditions are the key to everything. These are the recurring activities that can be anticipated and enjoyed throughout the year. My husband, Jim, wrote the following in the introduction to *Let's Make A Memory*: "The great value of traditions comes as they give a family a sense of identity, a belongingness. All of us desperately need to feel that we're not just a cluster of people living together in a house, but we're a family that's conscious of its uniqueness, its personality, character, and heritage, and that our special relationships of love and companionship make us a unit with identity and personality." If you haven't done so already, get started now creating those sources of identity that help glue families together.

I hope you will find helpful suggestions and ideas in *Creating Family Traditions* that will enhance your family life together. Each item ends with a Scripture verse that puts the activity into its proper context. After all, we are commanded to "do all you do to the glory of God." Could there be anything more important in your world than pausing for such a purpose with impressionable children? I think not.

Holy Week

As you approach Easter time, walk through Holy Week with Jesus. Each evening read from the Bible the events that happened in Jesus' life that day. You might also want to watch the corresponding scenes from Franco Zeffirelli's Jesus of Nazareth.

Palm Sunday—Jesus Enters Jerusalem

Matthew 21:1–11

Monday—Jesus Clears the Temple

Matthew 21:12–17

Tuesday—Jesus Teaches

Choose a passage from Matthew 21:23–24:51.

Wednesday—Jesus' Death Foretold

The Scriptures say nothing about what Jesus did on this day.

Isaiah 53:1–12

Thursday—Jesus Celebrates Passover with His Disciples

(See the special Maundy Thursday tradition outlined on page 16.)

Matthew 26:17–30

Jesus Is Arrested and Tried

Matthew 26:31–27:26

Good Friday—Jesus Is Crucified (A suggestion for a Good Friday celebration for the family can be found on page 18.)

Matthew 27:27–66

Saturday—Jesus Lies in the Tomb

Again, the Scriptures say nothing, but talk about what the disciples...Jesus' mother...and Mary Magdalene and other followers must have been thinking and feeling....

Close each family devotional time with prayer and maybe a song of praise or a favorite Easter hymn.

Palm Sunday Brunch

Start a special tradition with this Dobson favorite! Serve these yummy apple muffins with orange juice, fresh fruit, scrambled eggs, and crisp bacon. Decorate the table with palm fronds and take time to read about Jesus' triumphant entry into Jerusalem (Matthew 21:1–11). Little did the crowd know that He would triumph over sin and death during this holy week!

They took palm branches and went out to meet him, shouting, "Hosanna! Blessed is he who comes in the name of the Lord!"

John 12:13

Apple Muffins

1 cup chopped apples (pared and thinly sliced before chopping)
1/4 cup sugar
1 egg, well beaten
2/3 cup milk
1/4 cup butter
2 cups flour
1/3 tsp. salt
1/2 tsp. cinnamon
1/4 cup sugar
4 tsp. baking powder

In large bowl, mix together apples and 1/4 cup sugar. Blend in egg. Add milk and butter; mix together lightly. Sift in dry ingredients: flour, salt, cinnamon, sugar, and baking powder. Mix together well. Spoon into greased or paper-lined muffin tins. In separate bowl mix together topping: 4 tbsp. melted butter, 2 tbsp. sugar, and 1 tsp. cinnamon. Add topping to each muffin. Bake at 350 degrees for 20 minutes. Makes 12.

Maundy Thursday Foot-Washing

The dry desert sand and the open sandals worn in Jesus' day did not make for clean feet. That's why the household's lowest-ranking servant would wash the feet of his master's guests when they came to visit. So get a basin of warm water and several dry hand towels and let God's Spirit bring to life an amazing moment from Jesus' last days.

+ Read together John 13:1–17 and talk about what Jesus did and why He did it. What did He want to teach His disciples?

+ Take off your shoes and socks. Then take turns washing each other's feet. Imagine what it would be like if your favorite Bible-study leader, your pastor, or your Lord Himself was on His knees before you washing your feet.

+ Once everyone's feet have been washed and everyone has washed someone's feet, talk about some of the feelings you had. Was it easier to wash feet or have them washed? Why?

+ Think about people in your life. Whose feet, figuratively speaking, need to be washed? Which of the ideas you came up with earlier will you do—and for whom—this week?

+ What kinds of things can we do today for one another that would be similar to washing someone's feet in Jesus' day?
    * Taking a meal to someone going through a difficult time
    * Mowing the lawn for someone who can't
    * Grocery shopping for an elderly person or shut-in
    * Taking someone's car in for an oil change
    * Doing repair work on someone's house
    * Giving someone a pedicure or shoulder message
    * Getting someone a cup of coffee or tea

He poured water into a basin and began
to wash his disciples' feet,
drying them with the towel
that was wrapped around him.
John 13:5

Jesus is the Lamb of God, the Passover Lamb who died as a sacrifice for our sins. This truth can come to life with your own family Communion celebration on Good Friday.

Preparation

+ Read about Passover in Exodus 12.
+ Discuss why Jewish families eat unleavened bread when they celebrate Passover.
+ Read about the Last Supper, Jesus' celebration of Passover with His disciples (John 13). You might also plan some family or personal devotions around Jesus' last words to His disciples (John 14–16) and His prayer for us (John 17).

Communion

You may feel that only a member of the clergy should administer communion. If so, invite your pastor and his family to join your family.

+ Use one loaf of bread or a single piece of matzoth and one cup so that the family may share "one body" and "one cup."
+ Read from 1 Corinthians 11:23–26.
+ Share the elements of communion. Hold the bread for the person at your side and say the person's name followed by "This is the body of Christ, broken for you."
+ Pass the cup, again beginning with the person's name. Then say, "This is the cup of the New Covenant, Christ's blood poured out for the forgiveness of your sins."
+ Thank God for His amazing grace! He gave the gift of His Son for the forgiveness of our sins and He has adopted us into His family.
+ Close by singing a favorite Easter hymn or praise song.

And he took bread, gave thanks and broke it,
and gave it to them, saying,
"This is my body given for you;
do this in remembrance of me."

Luke 22:19

A Family Seder Meal

When Jesus shared the bread and wine with His disciples at the Last Supper, He did so in the context of a seder meal. Step back into history with this special celebration.

Background

Do you remember when God called Moses to lead the Jewish people out of slavery in Egypt (Exodus 3)? Well, the Passover meal that Jesus celebrated with His disciples the night He was arrested—and that faithful Jews still celebrate today—dates back to that time.

The Egyptian Pharoah did not want to let his workforce, the Jewish nation, go. Not even a series of amazing plagues (water being turned to blood; frogs covering the land; gnats swarming Egypt; flies following where the gnats had been; livestock dying; Egyptians being struck by boils; hailstorms killing slaves, animals, and plants; locusts destroying whatever the hail didn't; and three days of darkness [Exodus 7–10]) could convince him otherwise—until the last one.

The worst plague came exactly as God had said it would: He visited every house and took the life of the firstborn son unless that family had marked the door of their house with the blood of a perfect lamb. If a family had obeyed God and marked their door, He would "pass over" that house, and no one in that family would die. Finally, Pharoah sent the Jewish people away. The exodus of about three million people began. God's people were no longer slaves!

Matzoth—Unleavened bread; available in Jewish delicatessens and most grocery stores.

Maror—Bitter herbs, usually freshly grated horseradish or other bitter, pungent vegetable such as an onion.

I Iaroseth—A mixture of chopped apples, nuts, cinnamon, and wine.

The shank bone of a lamb—A symbol of the lamb that was sacrificed for sins. Christians know Jesus as the perfect Lamb, God's sacrificial gift for the sins of all.

A roasted egg—A symbol of the free-will offering that was given with the lamb, a symbol of giving more to God than just what is demanded, of giving a gift of love. Jesus was God's ultimate gift: God's law demanded only justice, but with the gift of Jesus, God gave us mercy, love, and forgiveness as well as justice. (By the way, the best way to roast an egg is to put it in a 400-degree oven on a piece of tin foil. Leave it in until it gets brown, probably an hour or so. You could also hard-boil a brown egg.)

Parsley or watercress—Represents the continual rebirth of growing things because they stay green throughout the year. To Christians, this represents God's gift of everlasting life because of the resurrection.

Wine or grape juice—A symbol of joy. As the meal proceeds and each plague is mentioned, every person sips a little of the wine. This ritual means that until total liberation, joy was incomplete. At the Last Supper, Jesus explained that the wine represented His own blood, poured out for us. He knew He must die so that we could know the total joy of freedom and forgiveness.

Elijah's cup—A goblet of wine placed in the center of the table. This cup represented Elijah, whom the Israelites believed would foretell the coming of the Messiah. This cup remains full to welcome Elijah and his announcement of the Messiah's coming. Christians believe that John the Baptist was this "Elijah" (Matthew 11:14). For Christians, this cup does not remain untouched, but it is used for Communion and shared by everyone at the table in the joy that our hope has come true. The Messiah has come to us and is alive to give our lives eternal joy.

The Meal

To remember this miraculous act of the Lord's deliverance, Jews share in a Passover seder meal. The head of the family sits at the head of the table. The dishes to be served should be within that person's reach so they can be passed to the family. A special dialogue between the youngest child and the father or grandfather, mother or grandfather accompanies the serving of these special foods (see sidebar where "elder" stands for "head of the family"). The dialogue has been adapted for Christians (see italicized lines at the end of each of the elder's statements).

Child: "Why is this night different from all other nights?"

Elder: serving the unleavened bread: "For on other nights we eat bread, but tonight we eat only *matzoth*. This unleavened bread reminds us of when our ancestors had to flee Egypt; they didn't have time to wait for yeast bread to rise. They had to be ready to move when God said so. *Like the Jews, we Christians must live so that we are always ready to go when Jesus returns. Also, yeast sometimes represented the evil in the world. God wants His people to be pure.*"

Celebrate the Passover to the LORD your God as it is written in this Book of the Covenant.

2 Kings 23:21

Child: "Why is this night different from all other nights?"

Elder: serving the maror: "For on other nights we eat other vegetables, but tonight we eat only bitter herbs. These herbs remind us of the bitter suffering our fathers and grandfathers knew when they were slaves in Egypt. *Likewise, many Christians have suffered so that you and I may know the joyous good news of Jesus. We remember the bitterness of their suffering.*"

Child: "Why is this night different from all other nights?"

Elder: passing the saltwater and parsley, followed by the haroseth: "For on other nights we do not dip our vegetables even once; but tonight—we dip twice. The saltwater represents tears of sorrow, and the parsley represents new life. We dip the parsley into the saltwater to remind us of the tears and the sacrifice necessary for springtime and new life."

"Next we dip the bitter herbs into the sweet haroseth, reminding us that the sacrifice was sweetened by freedom. Also, the color of the haroseth reminds us of the mortar the Jewish slaves used to erect buildings for their Egyptian masters."

Child: "Why is this night different from all other nights?"

Elder: "For all other nights we eat sitting up, but tonight we all recline. In the old days free men sat on soft chairs or couches, but servants had to stand before their masters or, while eating, sit on a hard bench. Tonight we celebrate our deliverance and freedom, so we sit in comfort and enjoy our freedom, wishing the same for all people."

Christians end the meal with Communion and an explanation that we are all God's "chosen people" if we have been "born" into God's family by believing in His Son, Jesus, our Messiah. As God's people, then, we should share the cup of joy with others out of gratitude that Jesus became the final "Lamb" to be sacrificed in order that "our joy may be full."

Easter Saturday

Celebrate early! Kids don't mind!

- In preparation for the big hunt, gather plastic eggs.
- Inside some of the eggs put candy or little toys.
- Inside other eggs put items that point to an event from Holy Week:

  A small piece of soap (John 13:4–10)

  Palm branch (Mark 11:7–8)

  Donkey (Matthew 21:1–9)

  Three dimes (Matthew 26:14–15, 46–50; 27:1–5)

  Picture of praying hands (Mark 14:32–42)

  Rooster (Luke 22:61)

  Purple cloth (John 19:2)

  Leather strip (John 19:1–15)

  A thorny stick (Matthew 27:29)

  White cloth (Luke 22:64)

  A die (John 19:23–25)

  Spear (John 19:32–34)

  Piece of gauze (Matthew 27:57–61)

  Stone (Matthew 28:1–2)

  Spices (Luke 23:56)

  Empty egg (Matthew 28:5–8)

Resurrection Eggs are available at local Christian bookstores as well as online at www.familylife.com/eggs/. Eleven eggs hold some of the symbols listed above, and one is empty, representing the tomb on Easter morning.

- Hide all the Easter eggs.
- After all the eggs are found, have the kids open their eggs. Talk about why they found a tiny bunny, a silk flower, silver coins, a tiny donkey, or a completely empty egg!

"Symbols of Easter"

Spring—Easter and spring go together. As the snow melts, buds appear on trees and seeds send their shoots up toward the sunlight as the deadened world of winter awakens with newness of life. Christians celebrate the new life that is available to them because Jesus rose from the dead.

Baby bunnies, chicks, and birds—Newborn animals remind us of the new and eternal life available to us because Jesus defeated death and rose from the grave. Also, because of that triumph, we can become new creatures in Him.

Green, yellow, pink, and purple—The colors of the Easter season are the colors of springtime flowers: New life appears where there once was death! Green specifically stands for new life, and purple, the color of royalty, reminds us that Jesus is King of kings and Lord of lords.

New clothes—A new Easter outfit symbolizes putting away winter and can remind us that God dresses up the earth in the lovely colors of spring. Also, because Christ rose from the tomb, we may live a new life.

Eggs—In eggs, like in Jesus' tomb, life is sealed away for a time. But then that life bursts forth just as Jesus burst forth from the grave! In Jewish tradition, eggs also symbolize a free-will offering, the giving of more than is demanded. Jesus is God's free-will offering: God gives us far beyond what we deserve or even dare to ask Him for. Jesus is the gift not only of life, but of eternal life!

Easter Sunrise Service

Plan Ahead!

Take some time to find a quiet, pretty place where you can sit and watch the sun rise. Prepare a simple, carry-along breakfast of hard-boiled eggs, rolls, and juice. Don't forget your Bible so you can read the Easter story together. You might even want to bring song sheets to sing some Easter hymns. (How can you celebrate Easter without singing "Christ the Lord Is Risen Today"?!)

Christ the Lord is risen today, Alleluia!
Earth and heaven in chorus say, Alleluia!
Raise your joys and triumph high, Alleluia!
Sing, ye heavens, and earth reply, Alleluia! (vs.1)
Soar we now where Christ has led, Alleluia!
Following our exalted Head, Alleluia!
Made like him, like him we rise, Alleluia!
Ours the cross, the grave, the skies, Alleluia! (vs. 4)

Alleluia... He is Risen

He Is Risen!

Get up early enough to get to your special place just before the sun comes up. Spread out a blanket to sit on. Then read together about the women going to Jesus' tomb and what happened when they arrived (Matthew 28:1–15). As the sun comes up over the horizon, sing a joyous song of victory! Then thank God for the gift of Jesus and His triumph over sin and death! Thank Him for the promise and hope of eternal life! Celebrate by sharing the simple breakfast you've brought with you.

Resurrection Buns

Just like the tomb on Easter Sunday, these tasty buns are empty on the inside! Enjoy!

1 package Rhodes frozen Rolls
24 large marshmallows
1/4 cup (1/2 stick) melted butter or margarine
1/2 cup sugar mixed with 1/2 teaspoon cinnamon

Thaw 24 rolls. Flatten each roll to about 3" in diameter. Place a large marshmallow in the center of the dough and pinch dough together to seal the marshmallow inside. Roll between the palms of your hands into the size of a golf ball. Dip in the melted butter, then roll in the cinnamon-sugar and place on a lightly greased cookie sheet spaced apart evenly. Let rise until double in size (30 to 60 minutes). Bake at 350º F for 15 to 20 minutes, until golden brown. Remove from the cookie sheet and cool on a wire rack.

May Day Morning Surprise

Make the first morning in May a special one for a friend, a neighbor, or a teacher. Start by crafting a May Day basket or use a basket you already have. Pick a bouquet of spring flowers—daffodils, tulips, whatever is blooming in your garden! Put the bouquet in a basket and hang it on the doorknob of someone you want to surprise. A basket can also be delivered with a smile to a teacher or secretary or coworker!

It is good to proclaim
your unfailing love in the morning.

Psalm 92:2, NLT

It's time to get dirt under those fingernails! Make planting a new garden a springtime family project!

- What do you want to plant?
- Where will you plant what?
- Will there be vegetables (no lima beans!!!) in one corner of the yard and flowers all around?
- What kind of special care do the bulbs need?

Buy the seeds, prepare the soil, plant the seeds, and plan for their care and feeding. Who will water and weed—and when? Now enjoy for months to come the fruit—and flowers and vegetables—of your labor!

> "What is the kingdom of God like?...
> It is like a tiny mustard seed planted in a garden;
> it grows and becomes a tree,
> and the birds come and find shelter among its branches."
> Luke 13:18–19, NLT

Turn "Outings" into Traditions

+ Gather the family and go on an annual spring picnic at your favorite outdoor spot—even if it's your backyard!

+ Each spring, adopt a family or neighbor that needs help with home or yard repair. Make it a family project with tasks for each family member to work on. And bring a plate of cookies when you go so you can visit a while, too!

+ Buy a lily during each Easter celebration. When the season has passed, plant the lily in a flower bed in your yard or the yard of a shut-in. Watch your lily patch grow bigger and more beautiful each year!

+ Go for a spring drive in the country. Look for as many new "babies" as you can find, like calves, foals, puppies, kittens, and lambs. Celebrate the new life that accompanies the season.

You have been born again…through the living and enduring word of God.
1 Peter 1:23

The Last Day of School

Make it a tradition to do something special on the last day of school!

+ Go out for ice cream at the end of the day.
+ Take the season's first swim. (Swimming at night is great fun!)
+ Hang "Welcome, Summer!" banners around the house.
+ Buy some brightly colored sandals or flip-flops.
+ Fill a piece of poster board with ideas of things you want to be sure to do this summer—places to go, things to do, and people to see. Use stickers as well as words and drawings to share your plans for "The Summer of 20XX"!
+ Have a big sleepover to celebrate the end of another school year.
+ Enjoy lemonade and Summer Lollipop Cookies (recipe follows).

Summer Lollipop Cookies

Make your favorite crispy-cookie dough. Refrigerate it for thirty minutes before rolling it out so that it's easier to handle.

Roll out the dough (not too thin) and cut it into round shapes with a cookie cutter or glass.

Place the cookies on a baking sheet and insert a wooden craft stick one or two inches into the base of each circle.

After baking and after the cookies have cooled—frost them with a sunshine-yellow icing.

Use candy or raisins to give your summer suns happy faces.

Serve with lemonade.

Photo Documentation: Good Time Had by All!

What if Lewis and Clark hadn't kept a *journal* on their western adventure? What if Ansel Adams had never taken his camera to Yosemite? We all would have lost out. So follow in their footsteps and be sure to pack a pad of paper, a pencil, and a disposable camera for your family's summertime adventures!

Take notes along the way. Did you stop at the best pizza parlor ever? What animals were you so surprised to see when you camped? Whom did you visit? What games did you play in the car? How was the plane flight? What did you learn about the place you visited? What did you see in the museum that you don't think you'll ever forget?

And take some pictures too! Then, once you get home and have the film developed, match the words and the photos, and you'll have a vacation journal to look back on for years to come!

The Lord is the Spirit,
and where the Spirit of the Lord is, there is freedom.

2 Corinthians 3:17

+ Hang up the American flag!

+ Bake a 9x13-inch cake, and let the fun begin! The cake can be made into a flag with a square of blueberries in the top left-hand corner and rows of sliced strawberries serving as red stripes. Kids can further decorate with red, white, and blue candles or small American flags on toothpicks.

+ Wear red, white, and blue. Add red, white, and blue crepe paper and construction-paper stars to a bike, wagon, or scooter you might be taking somewhere today. And if there's nowhere to go, how 'bout a neighborhood parade?

+ Sing "Happy Birthday to You" to America!

+ Catch a fireworks show in your area! It wouldn't be the Fourth of July without some "ooooohing" and "aaaaahing"!

+ Serve red punch with blueberry ice cubes! Fill ice cube trays with blueberries and add enough water to fill to the top. Freeze and *voila!* Blueberry cubes!

+ Talk about who founded our country, the Revolutionary War, and the meaning of the Declaration of Independence. Thank God for the blessing of living in a free country and for people who have died through the years to keep it free.

"This Land Is Your Land!"

Give a gift back to America by planting a tree or a bush in your yard or at a local government building, veterans' hospital, or public park.

- Discuss what kind of plant should be chosen for the spot you have chosen—and have received or will receive permission for!
- Talk about the positive results of giving such a gift: It releases oxygen into the atmosphere; it gives shelter to the birds; it provides beauty and shade, etc.
- Plan how to care for your plant if you will be planting it in your own yard.

Freely you have received, freely give.

Matthew 10:8

There's no better occasion for a potluck block party! Send out invitations early so no one misses out on the fun!

- Go all-American with your menu: hot dogs, hamburgers, potato salad, and baked beans. Apple pie and ice cream for dessert, of course!
- Decorate the tables with red, white, and blue napkins, plates, flowers, and tablecloths.
- While the burgers cook, have folks take turns telling who their favorite American hero is or one reason they're glad they live in America.
- Read aloud part of the Declaration of Independence.
- Sing some favorite patriotic songs together, ending with "God Bless America."

We have not received the spirit of the world but the Spirit who is from God, that we may understand what God has freely given us.

1 Corinthians 2:12

Family Reunion Fun

Does the second Saturday of August or the third Sunday in July work for you? Make it the same date every year!

- Reserve a good spot for picnics in advance and then let everyone know how to get to it and when to be there.
- Make it potluck! Have everyone bring a favorite recipe or one they're famous for. (Maybe this year Aunt Loretta will bring *two* blackberry pies so folks don't have to fight for a slice! But scheming for a slice is part of the fun!)
- Choose a different theme each year.
- Want crazy centerpieces for a farmer theme? Make a special flower arrangement to place on a red-and-white-checked tablecloth. Use craft foam for the flowers and pipe cleaners for the stems. Then crop and paste last summer's "reject" photos onto the center of the flowers. (Only use photos of folks who can laugh when they see themselves with their eyes closed, barbecue sauce dripping down their chin, or covered with goop after the egg toss.)
- Appoint a family photographer. (This honor can be passed along from year to year.) Have that person bring binders of the family reunion photos to the following year's reunion.
- It wouldn't be a picnic without an egg or water-balloon toss, or and egg-on-spoon relay. And, yes, adults participate!
- What about a hula hoop contest? And of course you need a football or two to pass back and forth.
- Bingo works, too! Don't forget the prizes!
- Plan ahead for the talent show of family skits, music, poems, jokes, whatever! Again, all ages are included!

- What special event can highlight your family heritage? If you're a Scottish clan, have a bagpipes player come. If you're German, take time to teach the younger generation the polka. If you're Irish, ask some local dancers to perform for you. If you're Greek, be sure to have some baklava to share.
- The grand finale could be the Family Presentation. The eldest member in attendance introduces the entire family to everyone attending. Everyone is introduced and, yes, it can be embarrassing. (Why doesn't Mom get our names straight?) But it's a great photo op and a way to meet new babies and new spouses.
- One more detail. Have a bucket on hand for donations for the next reunion. The funds cover the costs of mailing invitations and reserving the park.

Let us not give up meeting together,...
but let us encourage one another—and all the more
as you see the Day approaching.

Hebrews 10:25

Not All Sacraments Are Given in Church
—by Gloria

The hot sun bore down on the holiday beach-bathers lined up on their oversized designer towels. The smell of seaweed and ocean tides mingled with the sweet aroma of coconut oil and piña colada tanning lotion. The breeze was welcome, but not quite enough to cool the bottoms of feet baked by walks in the hot sand.

I was one of these overtired, over-scheduled escapees to the island. I was lying on my stomach reading a book when I felt a gentle sensation trickling over my feet.

"There," said Jesse. "I'm getting all the sand off, Mamaw. I'm washing your feet."

A quick glance over my shoulder and I saw my five-year-old grandson dipping water from a little green pail with his sand shovel, then pouring each measured portion over my sandy, burning feet.

"All clean, Mamaw. Now doesn't that feel better?"

The cool baptism was more than sacred to me. It had been only forty-eight hours since Jesse had been rushed by helicopter to Boston Children's Hospital. Suzanne had been the only one allowed to travel the thirty-minute trip with Jesse, her sweet boy confined in a neck brace and taped to a body board. I had followed by plane with Jesse's daddy, Barry.

It had happened so fast. Suzanne and seven-year-old Will had gone on to the hotel from the beach on their bikes; Jesse and Barry were to follow giving Jesse a bit more time to play in the waves. Riding home, Jesse got hot and thirsty and asked to stop for a drink. After waiting for a safe place to leave the bike trail to cross the busy road, they started across to the small store. "Come on, Jesse, let's go."

But for some reason Jesse was distracted and didn't follow right away. By the time he had started across, a car appeared around a curve going too fast for the busy holiday weekend.

Barry had watched in horror as the car struck his child. Like slow motion in a bad movie, Jesse's little body had been thrown into the windshield then hurled about 12 feet to land face down on the pavement.

"It's Jesse," the shaken voice had said on the phone when Bill answered the call.

"What is it, Barry? What's happened?"

"I think he'll be all right. Come to the hospital. Bring Suzanne. I couldn't get her on the phone."

Now we were moving like a bad slow-motion movie. Down the stairs, into the car, to get Suzanne and Will, through the tiny vacation-crowded streets, through the hospital corridors.

"It's routine. We have no pediatric unit here. We always life-line children to Boston."

But the reassuring tone in the nurse's voice wasn't nearly reassuring enough. We awaited every X-ray, every blood test, every CAT scan with an anxiety we weren't able to put at rest.

I stood with Will and Barry and Bill to watch helplessly as our daughter and her little son lifted off in the helicopter. She waved weakly from the window—a wave reminiscent of the one she gave as a child herself through the window of the tiny commuter plane the first time we all said good-bye to this island.

Over the years our family had kept up a love affair with this magical place, and now we had returned with a new generation to make memories.

But this was not the sort of memories we had hoped to make.

"Please, God. You go with them. Go with us all."

In a short time that seemed like an eternity we were waiting with Suzanne for more test results.

"Because of the mechanics of the accident, we need a few more pictures." We listened to that sentence over and over. With the return of each piece of film, each scan, each test, the doctors would shake their heads.

"You are a fortunate little boy," they would say to Jesse. "Tell all your friends to always wear their bike helmets like you did."

The doctors had wanted to keep him overnight, so we kept a vigil. He slept like a very exhausted boy would and awakened wanting something to eat.

By noon the next day we had landed back on the island and were walking across the tarmac to meet Will and his Papaw Bill, overwhelmed by the miracle of legs that move, eyes that blink, a giggle that escapes from a mischievous little grin, and a wide little hand holding tightly to ours. The next day we were lying on the beach again, and a little boy was baptizing my feet.

"Do this in remembrance of me."

Jesse hadn't come to quite understand those words yet. But I understood what Simon Peter must have felt when the pure heart of God knelt to wash his feet.

"All clean," said Jesse. "You're all clean now."

And by some miracle, I was.

- What would be a special "Good morning!" for the birthday person? Pancakes? Sugary cereal—just this once? Breakfast in bed? Not having to cook breakfast? If you're not sure, ask in advance!

- Choose one present to put at the birthday person's place at the breakfast table to be opened as soon as the special day begins!

- Mark the height of the birthday boy or girl on the garage wall or bathroom doorjamb—wherever you started that tradition. And if you haven't started that tradition, do so now!

- What does the birthday person want for dinner? Make his or her favorites!

- Before dessert or while you're eating the birthday cake, ask everyone at the table to offer an encouraging word about the person being honored: "Jon has sure become a much more confident reader"; "Sherry has worked hard all year at her free throws, and it's really paying off"; "I'm glad that Katie is making more time to read her Bible"; "Collin is being a lot kinder to his little sister"; "I'm glad Dad is my dad because I can talk to him about anything"; or "Mom's the best because she always knows just when I need a hug."

- Videotape an annual birthday interview of your growing child. Ask about special memories from the year. Be ready with prompts about happy times…challenges overcome…fun things that happened…accomplishments at school, in sports, in dance or music…and other meaningful moments. Add to this recording every year at birthday time! After the interview, play back the conversations from earlier birthdays and enjoy!

The Last Day of Summer

Make it a tradition to do something special and take the sting out of the last day of summer.

- Go out for breakfast. Look back at the summer and talk about all the special events (and even not so special) and thank God for the blessings and milestones.
- Buy a new lunchbox, backpack, and other school supplies you'll need.
- Go shopping for new school clothes and shoes.
- Take the season's last swim—and stay in until you're all wrinkly. Those homework assignments will get in the way of lazy swims.
- Bake a rectangular sheet cake. Cut it into the shape of a tombstone. Frost with white icing and, in black, write "R.I.P. Summer of 'XX." After this dessert, spend a few minutes praying about the new school year and all that God has for you.
- That "Rest in Peace" cake may be just the thing to share at the season's final overnighter—where there might not be a lot of resting, but there could be a lot of fun before the homework assignments hit again!
- Help your daughter/son make a card to give their teachers wishing them a good school year ahead.
- Have fun deciding together what to wear on that very special first day of school!

Turn "Outings" into Traditions

Have you ever noticed that if you do something once, the kids think it will happen every year? Well, capitalize on that charming trait and repeat these special outings every year. Why not let them be family traditions that everyone can look forward to?

+ Go to your family's favorite swimming lake or hole for a day/weekend.

+ Go inner-tubing together down your favorite lazy river.

+ Grab the fishing poles and head for a favorite fishing hole or plan a day on a deep-sea fishing boat.

+ Visit annual festivals in your area. Who is celebrating what? Join the fun! Is there a local arts-and-crafts fair? An annual Shakespeare festival? An open-air concert series? Plan to attend—and take a picnic!

+ How 'bout some summertime star-gazing? Make it a late-night adventure and drive away from the city lights so you can really see those stars!

"Can we do this again next Year?"

Labor Day

Just what kind of work have members of your family done through the generations? Make it a family project to find out and record what you learn!

- Interview older family members to find out about the kinds of work their great-grandparents, grandparents, parents, and they themselves did.
- What did Grandma and Grandpa like about their work? What made the work difficult? Why did they choose that line of work—or how did it become their life's work?
- Do a little Internet surfing or contact the family member who has already charted out the family tree (most families have at least one genealogist!). List the most famous—and infamous—"workers" in your family's history.
- Note those times when the need for work changed the course of your family's history. Did someone move west? What happened during the Depression? What did your grandparents do during World War II?
- What does the family's current youngest generation want to be when they grow up? What options exist that didn't for their grandparents?
- Thank God for making us in His image with the ability to work and be productive. Thank Him too for making each of us special and for showing us where and how He wants us to use the unique gifts and talents He's given us.

And who knows?! Maybe a younger family member will carry on the tradition of an older one!

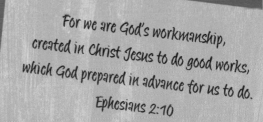

For we are God's workmanship,
created in Christ Jesus to do good works,
which God prepared in advance for us to do.
Ephesians 2:10

October: Clergy Appreciation Month

We always thank God,
the Father of our Lord Jesus Christ,
when we pray for you.
Colossians 1:3

In 1 Thessalonians 5:12–13, we are called "to honor those leaders who work so hard for you, who have been given the responsibility of urging and guiding you along in your obedience. Overwhelm them with appreciation and love" (The Message). Clergy Appreciation Month gives us an opportunity to do just that—and there are many ways to say, "Thank you!"

- Have everyone in the church—regular attendees as well as members, young and old alike—send cards to the pastors.
- Collect a love offering that your pastor can use for a special family vacation. Or use the money to get your pastor and his wife a weekend at a bed-and-breakfast.
- Offer free babysitting, call in advance and take over a meal, give a financial gift, or send a gift certificate from the local Christian bookstore or a favorite restaurant.
- Plan a cake-and-ice-cream social at church. During that time have several people share their words of appreciation and testimonies about a time when the pastor made an important difference in their lives. (Welcome humorous stories, too!)
- Encourage every Sunday school class to do something to honor the pastor.
- Do a "Thank You, Pastor!" bulletin board showing your pastor at your church through the years.
- Send a simple note of appreciation.
- Give altar flowers in honor of the pastor and his family.
- Most important of all, commit—or recommit—to praying regularly for your pastors. No gift is better than this!

Maybe you had the foresight in the spring to plant some pumpkins. But if a little patch isn't growing at your house, find a pumpkin patch nearby to visit. Decide in advance how many you'll be taking home and how you'll decide which one(s). (Does the youngest person's vote count twice?)

+ Enjoy a glass of crisp cider at the pumpkin patch. Drink theirs—or bring your own from home!
+ Find a good workplace at home: on the driveway, in the garage, or even in the house. Spread out several layers of newspaper.
+ Use permanent markers to draw faces on the pumpkins (a great and safe alternative for little ones!) or carefully carve your masterpiece.
+ When the sun goes down, place a lighted candle inside each jack-o-lantern you carved. Have Dad or Grandpa judge your handiwork for the funniest, neatest, and the scariest. Share mugs of hot cider and some freshly popped popcorn.

There is a time for everything,
a season for every activity under heaven....
A time to plant and a time to harvest.
Ecclesiastes 3:1-2, NLT

Jack-O-Lantern Munchies

If you carve a jack-o-lantern, try roasting the pumpkin seeds.

- Wash the seeds in a colander.
- Drain them on several layers of paper towels.
- In a large skillet, melt 2 tablespoons of margarine (butter scorches more easily). Add 1 tsp. salt.
- Add 2 cups pumpkin seeds and sauté about 3 minutes, stirring so that all seeds are coated with margarine.
- Place seeds on a cookie sheet and bake for about 25 minutes in an oven preheated to 300 degrees.
- Cool on a paper towel until pumpkin seeds are crisp and cool enough to eat.

- The Guest List: Be sure to include a few people around the table who have no family close by and nowhere else to go on Thanksgiving Day.
- The Menu: When you're planning your meal, call each guest and find out what one or two personal favorite Thanksgiving Day foods are. Do your best to serve one of each guest's favorites with your turkey.
- The Centerpiece: What will grace the center of your table each Thanksgiving season? Make both the decision and the execution an opportunity for family fun! Your project can be as simple or complex as you choose. Be creative. For instance, make pilgrim salt and pepper shakers, a papier-mache turkey, a dried flower arrangement, or a cornucopia filled with fresh fruits, vegetables, and nuts.
- "Thank You" Place Cards: For every person at the table, fold one unlined 3"x5" index card in half. Write each person's name on the front of the card. Decorate with Thanksgiving stickers or stamps or anything else you think of! On the inside write a personal message starting with a phrase like "I'm thankful for you because…." Make each message personal and specific. For example, "I'm thankful for you because you knew just what to say during those rough times this past summer" or "Thank you for always remembering my birthday."
- A variation on the theme: Use larger cards and have each member of the family write a message to everyone at the table. Each person will have a written hug from everyone else. It's fun to know what others appreciate about you—and it's good to slow down and tell people what you appreciate about them!

Two Kernels of Corn

After dinner dishes are cleared away, but before dessert is served, place two kernels of dried Indian corn in front of each person. This corn represents the first Thanksgiving: The Pilgrims had survived a very difficult winter and were thankful that God had brought them through.

Pass around a little basket. The person who holds the basket shares two blessings he or she is thankful for. There may not be a dry eye in the house after the basket has made its journey around the table.

> From the fullness of his grace we have all received one blessing after another.
>
> John 1:16

Thanksgiving at the Dobson's
—by Shirley

Thanksgiving is given major prominence in the Dobson home. It marks the beginning of the holiday season and the happy gathering with relatives who live close by. When the day arrives, excitement and anticipation fill the air. Wonderful mouthwatering aromas of turkey, dressing, and apple pies float from the kitchen as family members arrive. A new jigsaw puzzle is placed on the card table with a pot of hot coffee nearby. Various lawn games are set up in the backyard and a spirited basketball game is soon organized on the driveway.

When dinnertime is announced, we gather around the table and Jim reads a Scripture. Everyone takes the hand of the person sitting next to him or her and Jim prays a prayer of thankfulness to God. After the traditional meal has been eaten and the table is cleared for dessert, two kernels of dried Indian corn are placed beside each plate. I explain that this represents the first Thanksgiving when the Pilgrims came to America and endured such a difficult winter and how grateful they were to God for bringing them through. A little basket is then passed around and as each kernel is dropped into the basket, we describe two blessings for which we are most thankful. The comments invariable focus on loved ones, expressed with deepest feelings and appreciation. By the time the basket returns to where it started, people are usually crying. It happens every year. It's a time of affirmation when we share our need for one another and thank God for the family He has given us. This experience becomes more meaningful each year because of the inexorable march of time and its effect on the older generations among us. We have been painfully aware in recent years that some special people are now absent from the family circle, Jim's parents and my uncle. But we are grateful for each member of our small family who has survived another year.

I am reminded at this moment of a prayer expressed by Jim's father during the final year of his life. We had been to Kansas City for a visit and were on the way to the airport at the end of that pleasant vacation. Jim asked his dad to say a prayer before we were separated. I'll never forget his words, spoken in the car as we approached the airport.

He said, "Lord, we have enjoyed being together so much this past week, and You have been good to make this time possible. But Lord, we are realistic enough to know that life moves on, and that circumstances will not always be as we enjoy them today. We understand that a day is coming when the fellowship we now share will be but a memory to those who remain. That's why I want to thank You for bringing love into our lives for this season, and for the happiness we have experienced with one another."

Two weeks later, my father-in-law suffered a massive heart attack from which he never recovered. And his final prayer is his legacy to us today. Circumstances will inevitably change; nothing in this life is eternal or permanent. But while God grants us breath, we will enjoy one another to the fullest and spread our love as far and wide as possible.

Thanksgiving at the Dobson home is an occasion for the celebration of that philosophy.

I urge, then, first of all, that requests, prayers, intercession and thanksgiving be made for everyone.
1 Timothy 2:1

"I'm Thankful For…"

Can the family guess what Dad is thankful for in twenty questions?

The person who is "It"—in this case, Dad—thinks of one thing he is thankful for, and the others try to guess what it is by asking him simple questions Is it a person? Do I know that person? Male or female? Is it something that happened? Did it happen this year? Was I there when it happened?

If the group doesn't guess the blessing Dad has in mind, Dad wins the round!

> Enter his gates with thanksgiving
> and his courts with praise;
> give thanks to him and praise his name.
>
> Psalm 100:4

Who's Giving Thanks? We're All Giving Thanks!

After Thanksgiving dinner, give every person a piece of paper and have them write down three things they're thankful for. Place the papers in a basket. Draw them out one at a time and have the crowd guess whose blessings have just been read.

Thank You Lord...

Calling All Critters!
Decorate a Christmas tree for your furry friends

Look at the birds of the air;
they do not sow or reap or store away in barns,
and yet your heavenly Father feeds them.
Matthew 6:26

After the Thanksgiving dishes are cleaned up and while the football teams play on, welcome the Christmas season by decorating your first tree—for the birds and squirrels in your neighborhood!

Spread newspaper over your work area and arrange the ingredients for your gifts:

- meat tray of ground suet
- bowl of birdseed
- pipe cleaners
- peanut butter
- popped corn
- peanuts, unshelled & unsalted
- strips of colorful yarn
- crumbs from stale bread
- emptied orange halves
- pinecones
- cranberries
- raisins
- fifteen-inch pieces of floral wire
- stale doughnuts
- plastic knives

Now your gift-making can begin!

- Mix the ground suet with seeds or crumbs from stale bread. Fill the empty orange (or grapefruit) halves with the mixture. Attach pipe cleaners at three places around the edge. Join them at the center, twisting them together to form a hook so you can hang this feeder on a branch.
- Spread peanut butter with the plastic knives on the pinecones and then roll them in birdseed. Attach a pipe cleaner as a hanger.
- String cranberries, popcorn, and raisins on pieces of floral wire. Bend the wire and attach the ends to form a circle that you can hang on the ends of a branch.
- Tie peanuts along a piece of yarn and tie onto the tree.
- Tie stale doughnuts to the tree with yarn or pipe cleaners.

Have fun watching God's creatures enjoy your gifts to them!

What can you do to say, "I love you" in a special and maybe unexpected way on September 9?

- If Grandma and Grandpa are close, how 'bout a surprise visit? Or whisk them away for a special meal at your house!
- Have Mom or Dad take a picture of all you grandkids. Get it developed. Mount it with a wide enough mat so that you can write, "We love you, Grandma and Grandpa!" and sign your names.
- What are some of Grandma's favorite things to do with you? Make a date to do one of those.
- What does Grandpa like to talk to you about? Set apart some time to listen.
- What is one of your most favorite memories of time with Grandma and/or Grandpa? Let them know with a drawing, a photo, or a thank-you note.
- "I love you, Grandma/Grandpa, because…" could be the beginning of a note that special person will long treasure.

Their first responsibility is to
show godliness at home and repay their parents
by taking care of them.
This is something that pleases God very much…
1 Timothy 5:4, NLT

Turning "Outings" into Traditions

If it's worth doing once, why not do it every year?

+ Go apple picking at an orchard. Bake an apple pie from scratch when you get home with your sweet and tart autumn treats. Or make caramel apples. The possibilities are numerous!

+ Visit a pumpkin patch.

+ Ride your bikes together to a farmer's market and buy a variety of vegetables. Clean them together and cook in chicken stock. Bake some cornbread to serve with your homemade soup.

+ Catch a sunset—ideally on September 22, the first day of fall.

+ On the first Saturday of November, rake all the leaves you can into a big pile and invite the neighborhood kids to come over and jump in!

From the Hands and Heart

There's nothing like a homemade gift to make someone feel special! So, as the Christmas season approaches, plan a craft day—or craft weekend—and turn your kitchen into Santa's workshop. Your children will come to look forward to this fun time each year. Even shopping for supplies can be part of the fun!

Line a basket with Christmassy fabric and use your imagination to create "theme" baskets. The possibilities are *endless!*

♥ For the Movie Buff: A DVD of a favorite movie, a gift certificate for a video rental, a box of red licorice, and, of course, some microwave popcorn will mean fun at the in-house cinema!

♥ For a Special Lady/Daughter: Put together bubble bath or bath salts, a loofah, lotion, and body spray. Include a CD of soothing music, a small box of truffles, and a bottle of sparkling water. Top off with a single silk rose.

♥ For the Crafty: Gather supplies for that person's favorite craft (scrapbooking, tole painting, woodworking, stamping, etc.). Or— and this one's especially fun for children—include several large bars of Ivory soap, a small craft knife, and a booklet on soap carving.

♥ For the Fisherman: Fill a fish basket with miscellaneous fishing gear: fishing line, lures, bobbers, dry flies, cap, and, for those cold mornings— boot warmers.

♥ For the Chef: Accompany a special recipe—or recipe book—with several of the exotic ingredients that might not be on hand. Include a kitchen-related ornament. Top it off with a new apron that fits their personality!

Wrap each filled basket with a large piece of cellophane and tie with a big bow!

Use green-and-red plaid ribbon to tie a bundle of extra long cinnamon sticks together as an extra touch for decorating your packages.

Whatever you do, work at it with all your heart, as working for the Lord.
Colossians 3:23–24

Deck the Halls

- After bringing home the Christmas tree, serve the same dinner you served on the same day the year before (and maybe even the year before *that!*). You might have clam chowder and breadsticks; chili and cornbread; or lasagna and garlic bread! Play your favorite Christmas carols in the background, and be sure to end the evening with Christmas cookies and hot chocolate.

- Make a "Happy Birthday, Jesus!" sign for the front window! Year after year bring out that sign as well as any new ones you might make.

> "This will be a sign to you: You will find a baby wrapped in cloths and lying in a manger."
> Luke 2:12

- Arrange the nativity set together. Remember that Baby Jesus isn't in the manger until December 25—and those wise men start by being on the other side of the house and move closer to the stable as January 6 (Epiphany) nears.

- Hang a sprig of mistletoe in a doorway or archway. It's a great opportunity for family hugs and kisses!

- Tie curling ribbon onto cellophane-wrapped mints and hard candies. Then attach them using thin craft wire to a Styrofoam wreath for a sweet decoration! After Christmas, passersby can help themselves to a sweet treat!

- Have each member of the family whittle a Christmas symbol from a piece of balsa wood. Let each person explain what she chose (a fish, a cross, a manger, a star, a lamb, etc.) and what it means to her.

- Garlands for your tree, hallway, doorways, or stairway can be made from a variety of things: Cheerios; cranberries and popcorn; white Styrofoam packing squiggles; spray-painted uncooked pasta shapes; and Lifesavers!

- For a Lifesavers garland, cut two equal lengths of yarn. String the candy loosely on the first strand and lay it on a table so that the Lifesavers lie flat. Use the other piece of yarn to weave in and out in the opposite direction so that each candy is forced to lie flat. Remember to start stringing early!

- A chain made out of festive colored construction paper links can be a festive tool for counting down to Christmas! With each day, children can tear off a link and know they're one day closer!

A Little Tree for the Little Ones

There's nothing like a tree that children have decorated all by themselves! Sometimes that's the tree in the living room, but it could be their own tiny artificial tree for their bedrooms, the family room, or a playroom. That little tree will add Christmas fun to another part of the house, and it's a great place for some of the ornaments and crafts that come home from school and church.

If you...know how to give good gifts to your children, how much more will your Father in heaven give good gifts to those who ask him!

Matthew 7:11

A Growing Collection

Help your children remember each year's Christmas growing up by giving them each a special ornament—and do the same every Christmas season.

Is Jimmy into basketball and Katie excited about ballet? Maybe their ornaments this year could reflect those new passions.

Did Sandy start playing the trumpet or did the family visit Disneyland for the first time? The gift ornaments might mark those key events.

Was this the year Collin discovered cars in a big way and does everything Amanda wants have to have a monkey face on it? Find a Ferrari and a Curious George to hang on a branch!

Don't hesitate to let the kids choose their own ornaments.

Collections like these, with a piece added each year, will give your kids a good start on decorating their own family tree someday. Even more important, their collections will chronicle some milestones and memories from their growing-up years.

Gifts for Jesus

What can we give the One who gave His very life for us? We can give Him our life! And we do that by loving others with His love and by serving others in His name. So encourage acts of love, generosity, and compassion during this special season of the year.

Cut out a construction-paper Christmas tree or several holly leaves. Hang them on a window or door. Add a "Gifts for Jesus" banner above. When you see someone in the family loving someone with Jesus' love, grab a Sharpie and make a note of it. "Sarah helped her sister tie her shoes." "Steve brought in the trash cans without being asked." "Megan surprised Mommy with an unexpected hug and kiss."

> If your gift is to encourage others, do it!
> If you have money, share it generously….
> And if you have a gift
> for showing kindness to others, do it gladly.
>
> Romans 12:8, NLT

The Season for Love

- **Did you know that a shoe box can contain more than shoes?**
  A shoe box can contain practical items, fun treats, and, most important, lots of Jesus' love! Every year millions of children around the world receive a shoe box of love. People just like you and me fill a shoe box with things that a child—boy or girl, ages 2-4, 5-8, or 9-12—needs and wants. A toothbrush, comb, washcloth, new T-shirt, doll or car, hard candy, a ball, school supplies, a small stuffed animal—the possibilities go on and on. For information about where to send your boxes, contact local churches in your area.

- **Keep your eyes open for opportunities to buy gifts for** people in your community who are in need. Are the firefighters or marines collecting new toys? Is a local food bank asking for donations? Can your family adopt a family for Christmas through a church ministry or city hall? Or maybe someone you know is going through difficult financial times and you could be that family's secret Santa. Ask God to show you what He would have you do for whom! He'll show you, and you'll definitely be blessed as you are a blessing to others!

The Lord will reward everyone
for whatever good he does.
Ephesians 6:8

Caring Through Sharing

Sadly, for many people, Christmas doesn't mean having a lot of gifts to open. That's where you can make a difference. Early in December take some time to clean out your closet and toy box. Gather gently used toys, games, books, and stuffed animals that you can give to someone in need. Your church, maybe your school, and other organizations welcome such donations at Christmas. It's a great way for you to share the love of Jesus with others.

Each one must do just as he has purposed in his heart…for God loves a cheerful giver.
2 Corinthians 9:7, NASB

Tree Ornaments and Gift Tags

Hang these on the tree or use them to decorate packages.

+ Cut Christmassy shapes out of colored poster board and cover them with foil, or glue on glitter, buttons, or whatever is on hand to add pizzazz.
+ Make popcorn balls (recipe below) and then wrap them in foil or colored cellophane. Tie the wrapping with long pieces of colorful ribbon so that once you secure the popcorn ball, you can tie it onto the tree.
+ Cornstarch clay makes great ornaments! (Simple recipe follows.)

Caramel Popcorn Balls

8 cups popped corn (about 1/2 cup unpopped)
3/4 cup granulated sugar
3/4 cup brown sugar (packed)
1/2 cup light corn syrup
1/2 cup water
1 teaspoon white vinegar
1/4 teaspoon salt
3/4 cup butter or margarine

Measure popped corn into large bowl. Combine sugars, corn syrup, water, vinegar, and salt in 2-quart saucepan. Heat to boiling over medium-high heat, stirring frequently. Cook, stirring constantly, to 260 degrees on candy thermometer (or until small amount of mixture dropped into very cold water forms a hard ball).

Reduce heat to low; stir in butter until melted. Pour syrup in thin stream over corn in bowl, stirring until corn is well coated. Cool slightly.

Butter hands; shape mixture into 3-inch balls and place on waxed paper. Makes 16 balls.

Cornstarch Clay

2 cups baking soda
1 cup cornstarch
1 1/4 cups cold water

Pour ingredients in a saucepan and mix until smooth.

Bring to a boil for one minute, stirring until the clay is the consistency of mashed potatoes. While the dough is warm, divide into two portions (or more depending on how many colors you want). Use food coloring to make one red, the other green.

Pour the clay onto a cookie sheet and cover it with a damp cloth until it is cool. Knead lightly.

Once the dough is room temperature, roll dough on waxed paper and cut into Christmas shapes with cookie cutters. Poke a large nail through the top of each ornament to make a hole for hanging. Let them dry thoroughly, occasionally turning them over. For a final personal touch, glue on some glitter, baking sprinkles, or any other fun items you have on hand.

Note: Clay can be stored airtight in the refrigerator if not used immediately. Just warm to room temperature before using.

A Birthday Party for Jesus

Have a birthday party for Jesus! After all, isn't that what Christmas is all about?

Invite an older person who might otherwise be alone, a new acquaintance, the folks who just moved in down the street, a college student who's far away from home, and/or some people (pastors, teachers, Sunday school teachers) who are important to your family.

Decorate for the birthday party:

- Choose a festive table setting with lots of red and green, gold and silver. Have as the centerpiece a small wooden box full of clean straw and surrounded by three packages that represent gold, frankincense, and myrrh.
- Make "Happy Birthday, Lord Jesus!" place cards. Bake a special star-shaped cake in Jesus' honor.
- Talk about the significance of the wise men's gifts, and don't forget to sing "Happy Birthday"!

> They opened their treasures and presented him with gifts of gold and of incense and of myrrh.
>
> Matthew 2:11

Gifts with Meaning

- **Gold** symbolizes God's most precious gift to us—His Son. This financial gift may have enabled Joseph, Mary, and Baby Jesus to flee to Egypt when Herod ordered all babies killed.
- **Frankincense** was burned in Jewish rituals (see the word "incense" inside it?). The frankincense may have hinted at the fulfillment of the old Law: Jesus was the perfect Lamb sacrificed for our sins.
- **Myrrh** was used as a burial spice. Mary may have kept these precious spices and used them to embalm the body of her son, our Lord, thirty-three years after His birth.

More Christmas Traditions to Try

+ Make time each Christmas season to look back at family photos and videos. (You might just focus on photos and videos of Christmases past!) It's fun to share family memories and see how everyone has changed.
+ On December 1—or even on Thanksgiving weekend when the football games are on—set up a card table with a jigsaw puzzle. Find one that's hard enough to keep visitors and family members pleasantly challenged until Christmas—and that probably means one thousand pieces! See if you can find a Christmas theme or a winter scene.
+ Give each of your elementary-aged children some money with which to buy presents for family members.
+ Go Christmas caroling with another family!
+ Have a Christmas open house. It's a great way to see people who may be in town for the holiday! Choose a day and invite over your former Sunday-school class, youth group, swim team, neighbors, or officemates to come by between noon and three or four. Put a turkey in the oven early in the morning. Set out Christmas cookies and some orange slices and raw veggies to munch. Carve the bird and let people make turkey sandwiches and visit. Let everyone who comes know "Same time next year!"

> How good it is to sing praises to our God, how pleasant and fitting to praise him!
>
> Psalm 147:1

Christmas Card Connections

- Christmas Card Prayers

  After dinner but before people are excused, read aloud the Christmas cards that arrived that day. Take a few minutes to pray for the senders. Then display the cards on the fireplace mantel or hang them around a doorway, on the back of a door, or on the Christmas tree. Send a postcard to the family to tell them about your Christmas-card prayers for them.

- When you address the cards you're sending, be sure to say a prayer as you seal the envelope and put on the stamp. At mealtime, let your family know which cards went out that day so that they can join you in your prayers for those families.

> They all joined together constantly in prayer.
> Act 1:14

- After-Christmas Cards

  Don't let the prayers stop once the Christmas decorations are put away! In February pass around the basket of Christmas cards and choose a few from the collection. Once again pray for the families who sent the cards. If you weren't able to get a note off to those families in December, drop them a line now. What a great Valentine "I love you" for those families!

Memories of a Special Christmas—by Gloria

If everything special and warm and happy in my formative years could have been consolidated into one word, that word would have been *Christmas*. So, by the time the building blocks of my days had piled themselves into something as formidable as late adolescence, Christmas had a lot to live up to.

Christmas, by then, meant fireplaces and the bustle of a big excited family, complete with aunts, uncles, and cousins. It meant great smells from the kitchen—homemade bread and cranberries bubbling on the stove, pumpkin pies, and turkey. It meant Grandma's cheery voice racing to be the first to holler "Christmas Gifts!" as we came in the door. It meant real cedar Christmas trees, handmade foil ornaments, and lots of secrets. It meant enfolding in the arms of our great family the lonely or forsaken of our village who had no place to go. It meant all the good and lovely things we said about Christmas being in the heart and the joy being in the giving.

Then came that one year.

There were many things that conspired, as it were, to bring me to the laboratory situation in which I would test all my so glibly accepted theories. Grandma was gone, leaving in my heart a vacuum that wouldn't go away. My sister was married now and had the responsibility of sharing her holidays with her husband's family. The other relatives were far away. After a lifetime of serving in the ministry, that year Daddy felt directed to resign the pastorate of his flock with no other pastures in mind and "wait on the Lord." Since I was away at college, just beginning my first year, I wasn't there when my parents moved from the parsonage to the tiny cottage at the lake which a concerned businessman had helped them build. Nor was I prepared that winter day for the deserted barrenness that can be found in resort areas built only for summertime fun.

There was no fireplace. There was no bustle of a big excited family. Gone was the sense of tradition and history that is the art of the aged to provide, and gone was the thrill of the immediate future that comes with the breathless anticipation of children.

The dinner was going to be small, for just the three of us, and there wasn't any ring in the brave attempt at shouting "Christmas Gift!" that Mother made as I came in the door. Daddy suggested that because I'd always loved it, he and I should go to the woods to cut our own tree. I knew that now, of all times, I could not let my disappointment show. I put on my boots and my cheeriest face, and off through the knee-deep snow we trudged into the Michigan woods. My heart was heavy, and I knew Mother was back at the stove fighting back the tears for all that was not there.

There was a loveliness as the forest lay blanketed in its heavy comforter of snow, but there was no comforter to wrap around the chill in my heart. Daddy whistled as he chopped the small cedar tree. (He always whistled when there was something bothering him.) As the simple tuneless melody cut through the silent frozen air, I got a hint of the silent burdens adults carry, and for the first time felt myself on the brink of becoming one. So as I picked up my end of the scraggly, disappointingly small cedar, I also picked up my end of grownup responsibility. I felt the times shift. I was no longer a child to be sheltered and cared for and entertained. My folks had put good stuff in me. Now as I trudged back through the snow, watching the back of my father's head, the wary curve of his shoulders, his breath making smoke signals in the morning air, I vowed to put some good stuff back into their lives.

The day was somehow different after that. We sat around our little tree stringing cranberries and making foil cut-outs. But this time it was not the activity of a child, but sort of a ceremonial tribute to the child I somehow could never again afford to be, and to the people who had filled that childhood with such wealth and beauty.

The Night Before...

You can choose from among many activities to make the evening before the special day special!

- Attend a Christmas Eve worship service. Many churches have late-afternoon services that are kid-friendly, if not kid-led!
- Drive around and enjoy the Christmas lights decorating the homes in your area. Don't miss any award-winning neighborhoods!
- Sing Christmas carols as you sit around the fireplace, as Dad plays the piano or Big Brother strums the guitar, or in the car as you look at lights.
- Open your Bible and read about that first Christmas night when darkness became light with the sudden appearance of angels celebrating Jesus' birth (Luke 2:1–14).
- Let the children open one gift on Christmas Eve. A new pair of snuggly warm pajamas might be ideal!
- Sit around the tree with all the lights off except the tree lights and enjoy a cup of hot wassail (recipe follows).

Once the children are in bed, Mom and Dad share a few quiet moments together alone before calling it a night.

Hot Wassail

Mix together in a slow-cooker, pasta pot, or soup kettle:

1 part cranapple juice

5 parts apple cider (unpasteurized)

Wrap the following in a cheesecloth and tie off with a string to make a ball:

6-8 whole cloves

2 cinnamon sticks

1/4 chopped lemon including rind

Add the spice ball to the cider mixture.

Stir in 2 tablespoons honey.

Heat without letting mixture come to a boil. Leave on low heat and serve hot with a sliver of lemon or a cinnamon stick.

Making Christmas Morning Extra Special

It's finally here! Christmas morning has arrived! Get the camera or video recorder and let the fun begin.

You might want the first picture to be of the kids getting out of bed. Catch them as they walk into the room where the stockings are. Don't miss the moment when they see what's under the tree.

Now, it may be asking a lot to have the children wait to see what's in their stockings, so enjoy the laughter and surprises!

Before opening gifts, take time to worship God and thank Him for the Greatest Gift of all—His Son Jesus! Choose someone to read from Luke 2:1–20. Sing a favorite Christmas carol (or two!) like "Joy to the World," "Hark the Herald Angels Sing," or "O Come All Ye Faithful."

Keep the Christmas carols playing in the background as gifts are unwrapped.

When it's time for breakfast, try having the same special meal you had last Christmas morning—and the Christmas morning before that and the one before that! The menu might be blueberry muffins, scrambled eggs, and bacon; bagels, cream cheese, and orange slices; banana bread and deviled eggs; or an egg dish assembled the day before and baked while stockings are emptied.

Chipped Beef and Gravy

Two 4.5-oz. jars dried beef
  (I use Armour, which comes in a glass jar)
2 tablespoons butter
1 cup hot water

Pepper to taste
2 heaping tablespoons all-purpose flour
2 cups whole milk, plus a few tablespoons
more as needed

With kitchen shears, slice beef into narrow strips and place in a large skillet. Add butter and hot water, bring to a boil and cover. Reduce heat to low and cook for 10 minutes to coax the flavor from the meat. Season to taste with pepper.

Meanwhile, whisk flour and milk together in a medium bowl until smooth. Gradually add the milk mixture to the meat in skillet over medium heat, stirring constantly. Have extra milk on hand to thin if gravy thickens beyond the consistency of a creamy sauce. Add more pepper, if desired (you are not likely to need salt, as the dried beef is salty). Pour into a Christmas tureen or gravy boat and serve alongside a platter of hot homemade biscuits.

Gloria's Perfect Biscuits Every Time!

2 cups all-purpose flour
4 teaspoons baking powder
1 1/2 teaspoons salt

1/2 cup shortening (I use butter-flavored Crisco)
1 large egg
3/4 cup whole milk (as needed)

In a medium mixing bowl, whisk together the flour, baking powder and salt. With your fingertips or a pastry cutter, work in the shortening until the texture is like coarse crumbly meal.

Break the egg into a one-cup measure and fill the cup the rest of the way with milk. Add the milk and egg into the flour mixture and blend together just until all of the ingredients are combined. Don't overmix.

Turn the dough out onto a lightly floured cutting board. With floured hands, gently shape the dough into a circle that is about one inch thick. Cut biscuits out with a 2-inch biscuit cutter and transfer to a lightly greased 9-inch round cake pan. Re-roll and cut the extra scraps, being careful not to handle the dough any more than necessary.

Bake the biscuits in 350°F oven until lightly golden brown, 12 to 15 minutes. Serve hot with honey butter, chipped beef, or sausage gravy.

Let that cry of excitement prompt some "First Snow of the Season" festivities!

• Build a snowman—or a snowfamily—together! Be sure to take a picture of your new friends!

• Fill bird feeders for your feathered friends.

• Pop some popcorn, heat up some cider, and light a fire!

• Put the snow you shovel from the driveway and sidewalks in a big pile that's out of the way. When you're finished, reward yourselves by sliding down your snow pile on plastic sleds or inner tubes!

• Of course, what's the point of having snow without a good ol' *snowball fight?!*

New Year's Eve

+ Make a splash! Stay overnight at a hotel with a swimming pool! Go for a nighttime swim—the last dip in the old year!
+ Have a potluck party—with absolutely no Christmas cookies allowed!
+ Try fondue for fun! Make cheese fondue, beef fondue, and—everyone's favorite—chocolate fondue! Invite another family over to share!
+ Choose a favorite family game to play while you wait for midnight to strike! Maybe that's Monopoly, Yahtzee, Scrabble, Sorry, dominoes, Pictionary, Hearts, Spades, or Kadoo.

One more thing. It sometimes works just fine to ring in the new year with a city farther east. Folks in Florida can celebrate with revelers in Rio de Janeiro, and Californians can throw their confetti at the same time the folks in the Big Apple are watching the ball fall in Time Square!

New Year's Day

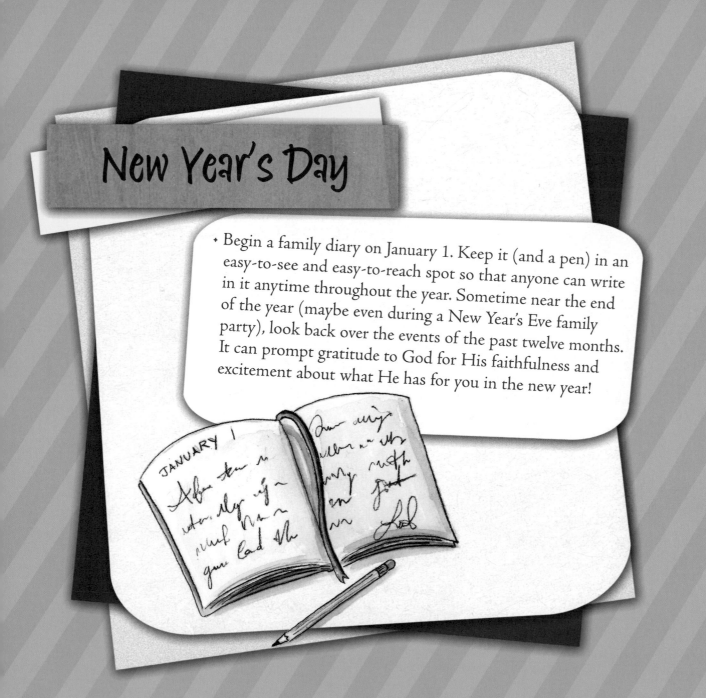

+ Begin a family diary on January 1. Keep it (and a pen) in an easy-to-see and easy-to-reach spot so that anyone can write in it anytime throughout the year. Sometime near the end of the year (maybe even during a New Year's Eve family party), look back over the events of the past twelve months. It can prompt gratitude to God for His faithfulness and excitement about what He has for you in the new year!

• Grab the calendar and designate one weekend during the coming twelve months for each child. On that weekend, let the child choose the activities and menus. Will it be a time for bicycling, skating, visiting the zoo, backpacking, eating Grandma's macaroni and cheese, or having dessert first? A weekend like this is a gift of family fun and of great memories for everyone!

• During the first week of the new year, plan some "Fun Family Nights"! Give every family member a different colored piece of construction paper and a 3"x3" cardboard pattern. Have each person cut out five squares and write on each square a family activity he or she would like to do on a family night. Put the pieces of paper in a basket or decorated jar. Each week draw one square from the can and do the activity listed. (The person whose color was selected one week does not get another turn until all the other colors have been chosen.) If you run out of ideas before you run out of weeks, take a "Fun Family Night" to add some more ideas to the basket or jar!

We Three Kings...

Do you know what January 6 is? It's Epiphany, the day we remember the wise men from the east arriving with gifts for the Christ Child. (Despite what we see in nativity scenes, the wise men weren't at the stable with the shepherds. These travelers from afar visited a toddler Jesus, not a newborn baby Jesus!)

To better remember these mysterious travelers, plan an Epiphany party!

Decorate with lots of stars, be sure to sing all five verses of "We Three Kings," and share a special meal. Chicken curry served over rice is one option from the east. (Sauces are available in the international sections of most markets.) Or you could make a meal fit for a king. That may mean prime rib—or calling out for your absolutely favorite pizza. For dessert enjoy vanilla ice cream topped with crunched up candy canes. And, oh yes, bathrobe attire is strongly encouraged! After you tie the belt around your waist, grab a backpack, put on your sandals, and wrap a towel around your head and pin a fancy pendant on the front. You are ready to journey to…the dining room! Happy Epiphany!

> After Jesus was born in Bethlehem in Judea….
> Magi from the east came to Jerusalem.
>
> Matthew 2:1

Valentines from the Heart

fold

Handmade cards are still the best! So head to the local craft store—there are all sorts of beautiful papers to make cards with. Or gather up white and red construction paper, lace, bits of ribbon or yarn, paper doilies, white glue, glitter, and crayons or markers.

Cut an 8 1/2 x 11 sheet of construction paper in half. Fold each half in half, and you now have two cards. Decorate the covers with the pretty craft paper, hearts, pictures, lace, doilies, or ribbons. On a separate piece of paper, write a poem or "three reasons I love you" for the person who will receive this card. Then copy it to the inside of the card. Or…there are some wonderful computer programs for making personalized cards that are simple and fun to use. After designing and printing them off, you can add more personal touches by adding ribbons, glitter, buttons, and lace, etc. When all is done, send your love, sign your name, and seal it with a kiss!

Valentine Surprises

Who will you surprise with a Valentine's Day "I love you"? Will Mom slide a note into the kids' lunch boxes or Dad's briefcase? Will Mom find a surprise love note when she gets into her car or opens the washing machine? Which elderly neighbor or widow at church would enjoy a red-and-white construction-paper hug? What single women could you kids send a valentine to? Be creative—and don't hesitate to let your computer be your friend! There are some great card-making programs available, and you could really spread valentine love around every year!

You're
Everything
to
me.

Let no debt remain outstanding,
except the continuing debt to love one another.
Romans 13:8

A Time for Just You and Me
—by Shirley

When Jim and I were first married, he was finishing his graduate training and I was busily teaching school. These career objectives forced us to postpone the experience of parenthood for a few years. We were extremely busy, but we were able to steal away for an occasional carefree weekend together. We would wander through department stores holding hands, laughing, and talking. We loved to window-shop for furniture and dream about how we hoped to decorate our house of the future. We would enjoy a light breakfast and then plan a candlelit dinner somewhere for the evening.

Many years have passed now—and such relaxing times are even more difficult to achieve. Although our children are grown now and live away from home, there are still the pressures of Jim's work. God has blessed our ministry far more than we ever dreamed possible, but the demands are many. We take several trips during a typical year but usually with obligations to be faced upon arrival. I must admit there are times when I long for just the two of us to get away again and spend a relaxed, self-indulgent weekend together. I remember one special time when we were able to do just that.

Mammoth ski resort was a six-hour drive from our house in California. After arranging for my mother to care for the children, we loaded the car and headed for our winter wonderland. I felt like a college girl again. We talked along the way and stopped to eat whenever it suited our fancy.

The next morning, we donned our colorful ski clothes and headed for our favorite restaurant, The Swiss Café. Hilda, the bubbly Swedish lady who owned the restaurant, called me "Shoooolie." During our visits there we had come to love her.

Our conversation at the breakfast table took us into each other's worlds, again. Jim's eyes never looked bluer, and the love that's always there between us, steady and committed, surged to an emotional peak.

Driving to the ski lodge was equally exhilarating. The roads looked like a Currier and Ives Christmas card. The giant evergreens appeared majestic in their white fur coats. I knew it was going to be a great day for skiing. The sky was blue and the snow was a skier's paradise. Once on the mountain, we swished back and forth across the mountain like two adolescents. The snow was so "forgiving" we could do nothing wrong.

We were wonderfully exhausted driving back to the condo. Jim prepared a cozy fire in the fireplace while I made our favorite meal of fried burritos. We set up a card table and ate dinner by the firelight, discussing the good and bad skiing techniques of our day and an endless variety of other topics.

After the dinner dishes were cleaned up, we pulled the pillow off the couch, chose some of our favorite records and put them on the stereo. While relaxing by the fire, we promised each other we would try to repeat this private rendezvous at least once a year.

Believe me, the memories of that weekend motivated me for days afterward to be the wife and mother I needed to be.

As important as traditions are in a family, husbands and wives need romantic involvement when they are alone—a time when the children are not even thought of.

This is good therapy not only for busy adults, but for their kids as well.

Flipping for the Family

Make heart-shaped pancakes! Prepare your favorite recipe or mix and then, as the pancakes come off the griddle, use a heart-shaped cookie cutter to make a special breakfast. (Breakfast can work as dinner, too!) Add fresh strawberries and sauce for a touch of red. Top off with a mound of whipped cream!

121

Dinner Is Served!

Hey, kids, how 'bout making Valentine's Day dinner for Mom and Dad? The company matters most (they'll have each other!), so don't worry too much about the menu (unless you want to!).

- Choose something that Mom and Dad like to eat and you like to make.
- Write up a menu using your best fancy-restaurant wording.
- One nice and easy idea is an assorted deli tray! Put together a platter of meats and cheeses. Don't forget mustard and mayonnaise, and you might want to have pickles and olives as well as some favorite rolls or breads. Arrange fresh fruit on another plate. Include a box of chocolates for dessert.
- Add some special touches like candles, linen napkins, and relaxing music in the background.
- You kids might even make plans to go to a neighbor's house or a friend's home so Mom and Dad can be alone. And…dinner is served! (Don't forget to clear the table and clean up the kitchen afterwards.)

Turn "Outings" into Traditions

What wintertime fun can become a wintertime tradition?

- Visit residents at a local retirement home.

- Pick a Sunday to work at a nearby soup kitchen.

- Go ice skating on a frozen pond or rink.

- Bundle up and go sing Christmas carols to the neighbors.

- Make and decorate Christmas cookies one afternoon. Package them into small individual servings, fasten them with ribbon, and bring them to friends and relatives.

- Volunteer to shovel snow off an elderly or disabled neighbor's walkway or driveway.

- Get a family gift wrapping assembly line together to wrap Christmas gifts, while listening to your favorite Christmas music. Each person can be in charge of a task. Mom can be in charge of measuring the paper. Brother can cut the paper, sister can fold, Dad can tape, and everyone can attach their favorite bow.